Glencoe Science

Chapter Resources

Geologic Time

Includes:

Reproducible Student Pages

ASSESSMENT

✔ Chapter Tests

✔ Chapter Review

HANDS-ON ACTIVITIES

✔ Activity Worksheets for each Student Edition Activity

✔ Laboratory Activities

✔ Foldables–Reading and Study Skills activity sheet

MEETING INDIVIDUAL NEEDS

✔ Directed Reading for Content Mastery

✔ Directed Reading for Content Mastery in Spanish

✔ Reinforcement

✔ Enrichment

✔ Note-taking Worksheets

TRANSPARENCY ACTIVITY MASTERS

✔ Section Focus Activity

✔ Teaching Transparency Activity

✔ Assessment Transparency Activity

Teacher Support and Planning

✔ Content Outline for Teaching

✔ Spanish Resources

✔ Teacher Guide and Answers

New York, New York   Columbus, Ohio   Woodland Hills, California   Peoria, Illinois

Glencoe Science

Student Edition
Teacher Wraparound Edition
Interactive Teacher Edition CD-ROM
Interactive Lesson Planner CD-ROM
Lesson Plans
Content Outline for Teaching
Directed Reading for Content Mastery
Foldables: Reading and Study Skills
Assessment
    Chapter Review
    Chapter Tests
    ExamView Pro Test Bank Software
    Assessment Transparencies
    Performance Assessment in the Science
        Classroom
    The Princeton Review Standardized Test
        Practice Booklet
Directed Reading for Content Mastery in Spanish
Spanish Resources
Guided Reading Audio Program

Reinforcement
Enrichment
Activity Worksheets
Section Focus Transparencies
Teaching Transparencies
Laboratory Activities
Science Inquiry Labs
Critical Thinking/Problem Solving
Reading and Writing Skill Activities
Cultural Diversity
Laboratory Management and Safety in the Science
    Classroom
MindJogger Videoquizzes and Teacher Guide
Interactive Explorations and Quizzes CD-ROM
Vocabulary Puzzlemaker Software
Cooperative Learning in the Science Classroom
Environmental Issues in the Science Classroom
Home and Community Involvement
Using the Internet in the Science Classroom

Photo Credits

Section Focus Transparency 1: Ron Watts/CORBIS; **Section Focus Transparency 2:** Museum of Paleontology, University of CA, Berkeley; **Section Focus Transparency 3:** Jeremy Stafford-Deitsch/ENP

Glencoe/McGraw-Hill

A Division of The **McGraw·Hill** Companies

Send all inquiries to:
Glencoe/McGraw-Hill
8787 Orion Place
Columbus, OH 43240

ISBN 0-07-825394-2
Printed in the United States of America
1 2 3 4 5 6 7 8 9 10 024 06 05 04 03 02 01

Table of Contents

Additional Assessment Resources available with Glencoe Science:

- ExamView Pro Test Bank Software
- Assessment Transparencies
- Performance Assessment in the Science Classroom
- The Princeton Review Standardized Test Practice Booklet
- MindJogger Videoquizzes
- Vocabulary Puzzlemaker Software
- Interactive Explorations and Quizzes CD-ROM with Presentation Builder
- The Glencoe Science Web site at: **science.glencoe.com**
- An interactive version of this textbook along with assessment resources are available online at: **mhln.com**

To the Teacher

This chapter-based booklet contains all of the resource materials to help you teach this chapter more effectively. Within you will find:

Reproducible pages for
- Student Assessment
- Hands-on Activities
- Meeting Individual Needs (Extension and Intervention)
- Transparency Activity Masters

A teacher support and planning section including
- Content Outline of the chapter
- Spanish Resources
- Answers and teacher notes for the worksheets

Hands-On Activities

MiniLAB and Activity Worksheets: Each of these worksheets is an expanded version of each activity and MiniLAB found in the Student Edition. The materials lists, procedures, and questions are repeated so that students do not need their texts open during the lab. Write-on rules are included for any questions. Tables/charts/graphs are often included for students to record their observations. Additional lab preparation information is provided in the *Teacher Guide and Answers* section.

Laboratory Activities: These activities do not require elaborate supplies or extensive pre-lab preparations. These student-oriented labs are designed to explore science through a stimulating yet simple and relaxed approach to each topic. Helpful comments, suggestions, and answers to all questions are provided in the *Teacher Guide and Answers* section.

Foldables: At the beginning of each chapter there is a *Foldables: Reading & Study Skills* activity written by renowned educator, Dinah Zike, that provides students with a tool that they can make themselves to organize some of the information in the chapter. Students may make an organizational study fold, a cause and effect study fold, or a compare and contrast study fold, to name a few. The accompanying *Foldables* worksheet found in this resource booklet provides an additional resource to help students demonstrate their grasp of the concepts. The worksheet may contain titles, subtitles, text, or graphics students need to complete the study fold.

Meeting Individual Needs (Extension and Intervention)

Directed Reading for Content Mastery: These worksheets are designed to provide students with learning difficulties with an aid to learning and understanding the vocabulary and major concepts of each chapter. The *Content Mastery* worksheets contain a variety of formats to engage students as they master the basics of the chapter. Answers are provided in the *Teacher Guide and Answers* section.

Directed Reading for Content Mastery (in Spanish): A Spanish version of the *Directed Reading for Content Mastery* is provided for those Spanish-speaking students who are learning English.

Reinforcement: These worksheets provide an additional resource for reviewing the concepts of the chapter. There is one worksheet for each section, or lesson, of the chapter. The *Reinforcement* worksheets are designed to focus primarily on science content and less on vocabulary, although knowledge of the section vocabulary supports understanding of the content. The worksheets are designed for the full range of students; however, they will be more challenging for your lower-ability students. Answers are provided in the *Teacher Guide and Answers* section.

Enrichment: These worksheets are directed toward above-average students and allow them to explore further the information and concepts introduced in the section. A variety of formats are used for these worksheets: readings to analyze; problems to solve; diagrams to examine and analyze; or a simple activity or lab which students can complete in the classroom or at home. Answers are provided in the *Teacher Guide and Answers* section.

Note-taking Worksheet: The *Note-taking Worksheet* mirrors the content contained in the teacher version—*Content Outline for Teaching*. They can be used to allow students to take notes during class, as an additional review of the material in the chapter, or as study notes for students who have been absent.

Assessment

ASSESSMENT ADVANTAGE

Chapter Review: These worksheets prepare students for the chapter test. The *Chapter Review* worksheets cover all major vocabulary, concepts, and objectives of the chapter. The first part is a vocabulary review and the second part is a concept review. Answers and objective correlations are provided in the *Teacher Guide and Answers* section.

Chapter Test: The *Chapter Test* requires students to use process skills and understand content. Although all questions involve memory to some degree, you will find that your students will need to discover relationships among facts and concepts in some questions, and to use higher levels of critical thinking to apply concepts in other questions. Each chapter test normally consists of four parts: Testing Concepts measures recall and recognition of vocabulary and facts in the chapter; Understanding Concepts requires interpreting information and more comprehension than recognition and recall—students will interpret basic information and demonstrate their ability to determine relationships among facts, generalizations, definitions, and skills; Applying Concepts calls for the highest level of comprehension and inference; Writing Skills requires students to define or describe concepts in multiple sentence answers. Answers and objective correlations are provided in the *Teacher Guide and Answers* section.

Transparency Activity Masters

Section Focus Transparencies: These transparencies are designed to generate interest and focus students' attention on the topics presented in the sections and/or to assess prior knowledge. There is a transparency for each section, or lesson, in the Student Edition. The reproducible student masters are located in the *Transparency Activities* section. The teacher material, located in the *Teacher Guide and Answers* section, includes Transparency Teaching Tips, a Content Background section, and Answers for each transparency.

Teaching Transparencies: These transparencies relate to major concepts that will benefit from an extra visual learning aid. Most of these transparencies contain diagrams/photos from the Student Edition. There is one *Teaching Transparency* for each chapter. The *Teaching Transparency Activity* includes a black-and-white reproducible master of the transparency accompanied by a student worksheet that reviews the concept shown in the transparency. These masters are found in the *Transparency Activities* section. The teacher material includes Transparency Teaching Tips, a Reteaching Suggestion, Extensions, and Answers to Student Worksheet. This teacher material is located in the *Teacher Guide and Answers* section.

Assessment Transparencies: An *Assessment Transparency* extends the chapter content and gives students the opportunity to practice interpreting and analyzing data presented in charts, graphs, and tables. Test-taking tips that help prepare students for success on standardized tests and answers to questions on the transparencies are provided in the *Teacher Guide and Answers* section.

Teacher Support and Planning

Content Outline for Teaching: These pages provide a synopsis of the chapter by section, including suggested discussion questions. Also included are the terms that fill in the blanks in the students' *Note-taking Worksheets*.

Spanish Resources: A Spanish version of the following chapter features are included in this section: objectives, vocabulary words and definitions, a chapter purpose, the chapter Activities, and content overviews for each section of the chapter.

Reproducible
Student Pages

Hands-On
Activities

Dating Rock Layers with Fossils

Procedure

1. In the space below, draw three rock layers.

2. Number the layers 1 to 3, bottom to top.

3. Layer 1 contains fossil A. Layer 2 contains fossils A and B. Layer 3 contains fossil C.

4. Fossil A lived from the Cambrian through the Ordovician. Fossil B lived from the Ordovician through the Silurian. Fossil C lived in the Silurian and Devonian.

Data and Observations

Drawing of rock layers:

Table 1

Period	Fossil		
	A	B	C
Permian			
Pennsylvanian			
Mississippian			
Devonian			↑
Silurian		↑	
Ordovician	↑		
Cambrian			

Analysis

1. Which layers were you able to date to a specific period?

_____

_____

_____

2. Why isn't it possible to determine during which specific period the other layers formed?

_____

_____

_____

TRY AT HOME

Calculating the Age of the Atlantic Ocean

Procedure

1. On a **world map** or **globe,** measure the distance in kilometers between a point on the east coast of South America and a point on the west coast of Africa.

2. Measure in SI several times and take the average of your results.

3. Assuming that Africa has been moving away from South America at a rate of 3.5 cm per year, calculate how many years it took to create the Atlantic Ocean.

Data and Observations

Table 1

Measurement	Distance (km)
1	
2	
3	
4	

Calculations:

1. Average distance = _____ km

2. Average distance in cm = _____ cm

3. Time (average distance in cm ÷ 3.5 cm/yr) = _____ years

Analysis

1. Did the values used to obtain your average value vary much?

_____

_____

_____

2. How close did your age come to the accepted estimate for the beginning of the breakup of Pangaea in the Triassic Period?

_____

_____

_____

 Changing Species

Lab Preview

Directions: *Answer these questions before you begin the Activity.*

1. How many times will you draw cards representing a pair of varimals that will mate and produce offspring?

   _____

2. Can you name another variable in your numbered playing cards and explain how that variable could model adaptation within a species?

   _____

   _____

In this activity, you will observe how adaptation within a species might cause the evolution of a particular trait, leading to the development of a new species.

What You'll Investigate

How might adaptation within a species cause the evolution of a particular trait?

Materials

deck of playing cards

Goals

- **Model** adaptation within a species.

Procedure

1. Remove all of the kings, queens, jacks, and aces from a deck of playing cards.
2. Each remaining card represents an individual in a population of animals called "varimals." The number on each card represents the height of the individual. For example, the 5 of diamonds is a varimal that's 5 units tall.
3. **Calculate** the average height of the population of varimals represented by your cards. Record your data in Table 1 of the Data and Observations section.
4. Suppose varimals eat grass, shrubs, and leaves from trees. A drought causes many of these plants to die. All that's left are a few tall trees. Only varimals at least 6 units tall can reach the leaves on these trees.
5. All the varimals under 6 units leave the area to seek food elsewhere or die from starvation. Discard all of the cards with a number value less than 6. Calculate the new average height of the population of varimals.
6. Shuffle the deck of remaining cards.
7. **Draw** two cards at a time. Each pair represents a pair of varimals that will mate.
8. The offspring of each pair reaches a height equal to the average height of his or her parents. Calculate the height of each offspring, and record your data in Table 2 of the Data and Observations section.
9. Repeat by discarding all parents and offspring under 8 units tall. Now calculate the new average height of varimals. Include both the parents and offspring in your calculation.

Activity (continued)

Data and Observations

Table 1

Varimal Population Height	
Cards used for calculating height	**Average height of population**
2 through 10	1.
6 through 10	2.
8 through 10 (Includes offspring from Table 2 who are 8 or more units tall.)	3.

Table 2

Varimal Offspring Height	
Parent cards drawn	**Offspring Height**
1.	
2.	
3.	
4.	
5.	
6.	
7.	
8.	
9.	
10.	

Conclude and Apply

1. How did the height of the population change?

_____

2. If you hadn't discarded the shortest varimals, would the average height of the population have changed as much? **Explain.**

_____

3. Why didn't every member of the original population reproduce?

_____

4. If there had been no varimals over 6 units tall in step 5, what would have happened to the population?

_____

5. If there had been no variation in height in the population before the droughts occurred, would the species have been able to evolve into a taller species? **Explain.**

_____

6. How does this activity demonstrate that traits evolve in species?

_____

Use the Internet
Discovering the Past

Imagine what the world was like millions of years ago. What animals might have been roaming around the spot where you now sit? Can you picture a Tyrannosaurus rex roaming the area that is now Dinosaur National Park? The animals and plants that once inhabited your region might have left some clues to their identity—fossils. Scientists use fossils to piece together what Earth looked like in the geologic past. Fossils can help determine whether an area used to be dry land or was underwater. Fossils can help uncover clues about how plants and animals have evolved over the course of time. Using the resources of the Internet and by sharing data with your peers, you can start to discover how North America has changed through time.

Recognize the Problem

How has your area changed over geologic time?

Form a Hypothesis

How might the area where you are now living have looked thousands or millions of years ago? Do you think that the types of animals and plants have changed much over time? Form a hypothesis concerning the change in organisms and geography from long ago to the present day in your area.

Goals

- **Gather** information about fossils found in your area.
- **Communicate** details about fossils found in your area.
- **Synthesize** information from sources about the fossil record and the changes in your area over time.

Data Source

SCIENCE*Online* Go to the Glencoe Science Web site at **science.glencoe.com** to get more information about fossils and changes over geologic time and for data collected by other students.

Test Your Hypothesis

Plan

1. **Determine** the age of the rocks that make up your area. Were they formed during Precambrian time, the Paleozoic Era, the Mesozoic Era, or the Cenozoic Era?
2. Gather information about the fossil plants and animals found in your area during one of the above geologic time intervals. Find specific information on when, where and how the fossil organisms lived. If no fossils are known from your area, find out information about the fossils found nearest your area.

Do

1. Make sure your teacher approves your plan before you start.
2. Go to the Glencoe Science Web site at **science.glencoe.com** to post your data in the table. Add any additional information you think is important to understanding the fossils found in your area.

Activity (continued)

Data and Observations

Table 1

Fossil name	Plant or animal fossil	Age of fossil	Detail about fossil	Location

Analyze Your Data

1. What present-day relatives of prehistoric animals or plants exist in your area?

   _____

2. How have the organisms in your area changed over time? Is your hypothesis supported? Why or why not?

   _____

   _____

3. What other information did you discover about your area's climate or environment from the geologic time period you investigated?

   _____

Draw Conclusions

1. Find this *On the Internet* activity on the Glencoe Science Web site at **science.glencoe.com**. Compare your data to those of other students. Study other students' data to compare information about the geologic time periods and fossils that you investigated. Review data that other students have entered about fossils they have researched.

2. **Describe** the plant and animal fossils that have been discovered in your area. What clues did you discover about the environment of your fossil organisms? How do these compare to the environment of your area today?

   _____

   _____

3. **Infer** from the fossil organisms found in your area what the geography and climate were like during the geologic time period you chose.

   _____

   _____

Differences in a Species

To use fossil dating efficiently, paleontologists first separate fossils into groups. The most useful group for classification is called a species. A species is a population of individuals that have similar characteristics. Small differences in individuals might result in the development of a new species by a series of gradual changes. These changes can be traced from one geologic time division to another if the fossil record is good.

Strategy

You will describe the variations present within a species.
You will describe a species in terms of one characteristic.

Materials

meterstick   graph paper   pencils (colored)

Procedure

1. The species you will study is *Homo sapiens,* or yourself. You and your classmates are all members of this species. Remember that all living things grow at different rates. It is possible that you will find some big differences in your study, but everyone still belongs to the same species.

2. Record all characteristics of the species that you can. Record which of the characteristics you could measure and compare for all members of the species.

3. Measure and record in Table 1 the height of yourself and each of your classmates. Round off the height to the nearest tenth of a meter (0.1 m).

4. Measure the heights of a class of younger students. Record this data in Table 2.

Data and Observations

1. Characteristics: _____

_____

Table 1

Name	Height (m)	Name	Height (m)	Name	Height (m)

Laboratory Activity 1 (continued)

Table 2

Name	Height (m)	Name	Height (m)	Name	Height (m)

Use a separate sheet of paper to graph the Frequency (number of persons having the same height) on the vertical axis against the Height (m) on the horizontal axis. Use one color for your own class and a second color for the younger class.

Questions and Conclusions

1. On what characteristics can you classify this group as a single species?

   _____

2. Where do most of the members of your class fall in regard to height?

   _____

3. Where do most of the members of the younger class fall in regard to height?

   _____

4. What change has taken place over time?

   _____

5. How is this activity like fossil dating?

   _____

   _____

6. How is this activity different from fossil dating? (Hint: Think in terms of the time spans involved.)

   _____

   _____

   _____

Strategy Check

_____ Can you describe the variations present within a species?

_____ Can you describe a species in terms of a range of a characteristic?

Looking at the Geologic Time Scale

As you have learned, Earth's history can be divided in geologic time segments called eras, periods, and epochs. These time periods are useful for placing events such as the disappearance of the dinosaurs and the appearance of humans in perspective relative to the history of life on Earth. The time segments are not as equal as they sound, however. In earlier eras, life processes on Earth appear to have been developing quite slowly, whereas later eras saw enormous changes over relatively short segments of geologic time. In this Laboratory Activity you will compare and contrast various segments of Earth's history by constructing a geologic time line.

Strategy

You will make a graph to compare the durations of Earth's geologic eras.
You will measure and construct a time line that shows Earth's geologic eras.
You will identify time relationships among events in Earth's geologic history.
You will record and illustrate significant events during the Mesozoic and Cenozoic Eras on a time line.

Materials

4–4.5 m of adding machine tape
meter stick
colored pencils

Procedure

Part A

1. Figure 1 shows approximately how long ago each major division of Earth's geologic time scale began. Use the information to calculate how long each of these divisions lasted. Record that information in the last column of Figure 1.

2. Using that information, make a bar graph on the grid in the Data and Observations section to show how long each division lasted.

Part B

3. You will use a piece of adding machine tape to make a geologic time line. Distance will represent time, with 1 cm representing 10 million years.

4. Using the meter stick, draw a straight line through the middle of the tape from one end to the other.

5. Starting at the left end of the tape, measure a distance that represents the length of Precambrian Time. Refer back to the time duration you calculated in Figure 1. Make a vertical line at the correct point.

To the left of that line label the division on your time line *Precambrian Time.*

6. From that vertical line, measure a distance that represents the length of the Paleozoic Era. Refer back to the time duration you calculated in Figure 1. Make a vertical line at the correct point. To the left of that line, label the division on your time line *Paleozoic Era.*

7. Repeat step 6 for the Mesozoic Era and the Cenozoic Era.

8. Lightly color each division on your time line a different color.

9. Divide the Mesozoic Era and the Cenozoic Era into the Periods and Epochs shown in Figure 2.

10. Then, using information from your text (such as the mass extinction) and the additional information in Figure 2, mark in the correct positions on your time line for significant events that occurred during the Mesozoic and Paleozoic Eras. Illustrate each of these events with a small drawing.

Laboratory Activity 2 (continued)

Data and Observations

Figure 1

Major geologic time division	When time division began	Length of time division lasted
Precambrian Time	4.5 billion years ago	
Paleozoic Era	544 million years ago	
Mesozoic Era	248 million years ago	
Cenozoic Era	65 million years ago	

Figure 2

Division	Time period (millions of years ago)	Event(s)
Triassic Period	248–213	breakup of Pangaea
Jurassic Period	213–145	first birds
Cretaceous Period	145–65	Rocky Mountains form; first flowering plants
Paleocene Epoch	65–55.5	first hooved mammals
Eocene Epoch	55.5–33.7	first whales
Oligocene Epoch	33.7–23.8	early formation of European Alps
Miocene Epoch	23.8–5.3	first dogs and bears
Pliocene Epoch	5.3–1.8	first Ice Age; first hominoids
Pleistocene Epoch	1.8–0.008	modern humans
Holocene Epoch	0.008–present	Sea levels rose as climate warmed; first civilizations

Laboratory Activity 2 (continued)

Graph

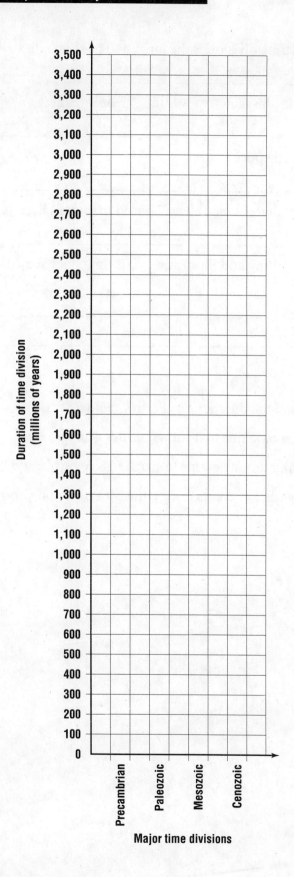

Laboratory Activity 2 (continued)

Questions and Conclusions

1. Based on your graph in Part A, which time division is the longest? The shortest?

_____

2. About how many times longer than the Mesozoic Era was the Paleozoic Era?

_____

3. In which era do you live today? In which epoch?

_____

4. About how many times longer than modern humans have hooved mammals lived on Earth?

_____

5. What problems did you have in constructing and illustrating your time line? Why did you have those problems?

_____

_____

Strategy Check

_____ Can you make a graph to compare the durations of Earth's geologic eras?

_____ Can you measure and construct a time line that shows Earth's geologic eras?

_____ Can you identify time relationships among events in Earth's geologic history?

_____ Can you record and illustrate significant events during the Mesozoic and Cenozoic Eras on a time line?

Geologic Time

Directions: Use this page to label your Foldable in the **Before You Read** at the beginning of the chapter.

Paleozoic Era

Mesozoic Era

Cenozoic Era

Modern horse

dinosaurs were dominant

era I live in

first fish, reptiles, amphibians, and land plants began to appear

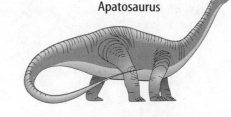

Apatosaurus

mammals began to dominate land

mountains like the Appalachian Mountains were formed

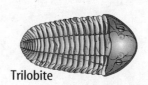

Trilobite

Rocky Mountains were formed

Meeting Individual Needs

Directed Reading for Content Mastery

Overview
Geologic Time

Directions: *Study the diagram. Then complete the sentences below.*

Precambrian time

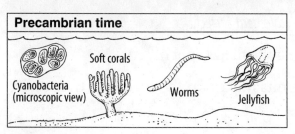

Cyanobacteria (microscopic view) Soft corals Worms Jellyfish

4.6 billion years ago ⟶ 544 million years ago

Paleozoic Era

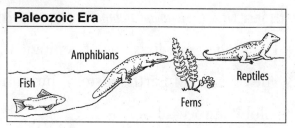

Fish Amphibians Ferns Reptiles

⟶ 245 million years ago

Mesozoic Era

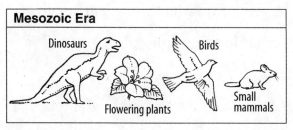

Dinosaurs Birds Flowering plants Small mammals

245 million years ago ⟶ 66 million years ago

Cenozoic Era

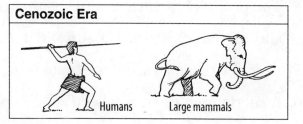

Humans Large mammals

⟶ now

1. Ferns and reptiles appeared in the _____ Era.

2. In the _____ Era, humans and large mammals appeared.

3. Dinosaurs, birds, and flowering plants first appeared in the

_____ Era.

4. During _____ time, the earliest life-forms appeared.

5. Small mammals appeared in the _____ Era.

6. The earliest life-form shown above is _____.

7. Reptiles appeared during the same era as ferns, fishes,

and _____.

8. Worms and jellyfishes first appeared in _____ time.

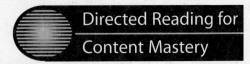 Directed Reading for Content Mastery

Section 1 ▪ Life and Geologic Time
Section 2 ▪ Early Earth History

Directions: *Circle the term in parentheses that makes each statement correct.*

1. The longest subdivisions of geologic time are called (epochs, eons).

2. The division of Earth's history into time units makes up the (geologic time scale, trilobite time scale).

3. A group of organisms that reproduce only with members of their group is a (population, species).

4. The process by which organisms that adapt well to their environment survive and reproduce is called (natural selection, organic evolution).

5. Pangaea formed during the (Paleozoic, Mesozoic) Era.

6. A subdivision of eras, called (epochs, periods), are characterized by the types of life existing worldwide.

7. (Fossils, Plates) help scientists divide Earth's history into time units.

8. The changing of organisms over geologic time is known as (natural selection, organic evolution).

9. The oldest rocks on earth contain (only a few, no) fossils.

10. The Precambrian time is the (longest, shortest) part of Earth's history.

11. Cyanobacteria are (colorless, blue-green) bacteria thought to be one of the earliest forms of life on Earth.

Directions: *Write **A, B, C, D,** or **E** beneath the proper illustration to show in which order they first appeared on Earth.*

Reptile	Cyanobacteria	Fish	Amphibian	Jellyfish
	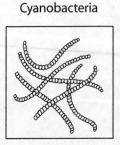	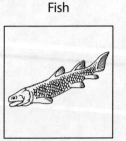		

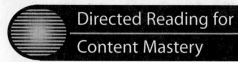 **Section 3 ▪ Middle and Recent Earth History**

Directions: *Use the following terms to fill in the chart below.*

present   birds   *Homo sapiens*   Pangaea

Alps and Himalayas   dinosaurs   angiosperms

Era	Time Span	Period	Life-forms	Geologic Events
Mesozoic	245 to 65 million years before present	Triassic	The first small 2. _____ appeared.	6. _____ separated into two large land masses.
		Jurassic	The first 3. _____ appeared.	
		Cretaceous	New plants called 4. _____ evolved.	
Cenozoic	65 million years before present to 1. _____	Tertiary	Dinosaurs became extinct.	7. _____ begin to rise. Ice Age began.
		Quarternary	5. _____ appeared.	Ice ages begin.

Directions: *For each of the following, write the letter of the term or phrase that best completes the sentence.*

_____ **8.** The Mesozoic Era is also known as the era of _____.
   a. middle life   **b.** new life

_____ **9.** Birds appeared during the _____ Period.
   a. Triassic   **b.** Jurassic

Directed Reading for Content Mastery

Key Terms
Geologic Time

Directions: *Draw a line to connect the description on the left to the correct term on the right.*

1. major subdivisions of geological time based on differences in life-forms

2. organisms that lived hundreds of millions of years ago with bodies divided into three sections

3. the longest geological part of Earth's history

4. one of the earliest life-forms, which gave off oxygen

5. flying animals that evolved from dinosaurs

6. the single landmass that once contained all Earth's continents

7. smaller units of time in a geologic period

8. the time period where dinosaurs were the dominant life-form

9. the division of Earth's history into time units

10. the longest subdivisions of geologic time

11. major divisions of an era

12. the change in organisms over time

13. a group of organisms that normally reproduce with other members of their group

14. process by which certain organisms survive and reproduce

Precambrian

geologic time scale

eras

species

trilobites

periods

Pangaea

natural selection

cyanobacteria

eons

birds

organic evolution

Jurassic

epoch

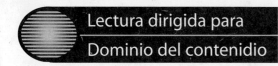

Lectura dirigida para Dominio del contenidio

Sinopsis
El tiempo geológico

Instrucciones: *Estudia el diagrama y completa las oraciones.*

Tiempo Precámbrico

Corales blandos

Cianobacterias (vista microscóspica)

Gusanos

Aguamalas

hace 4.6 billones de años ⟶ hace 544 millones de años

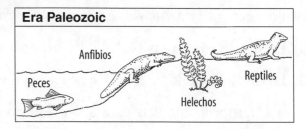

Era Paleozoic

Anfibios

Peces

Helechos

Reptiles

⟶ hace 245 millones de años

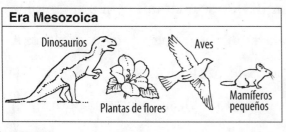

Era Mesozoica

Dinosaurios

Aves

Plantas de flores

Mamíferos pequeños

hace 245 millones de años ⟶ hace 66 millones de años

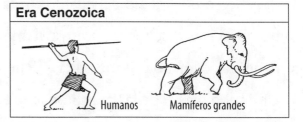

Era Cenozoica

Humanos

Mamíferos grandes

⟶ presente

Satisface las necesidades individuales

1. Los helechos y los reptiles aparecieron en la Era _____.

2. En la Era _____ hicieron su debut los seres humanos y los mamíferos grandes.

3. Dinosaurios, aves y plantas con flores aparecieron en la Era _____.

4. Durante el tiempo _____, aparecieron las formas más primitivas de vida.

5. En la Era _____ aparecieron por primera vez animales pequeños.

6. Las formas de vida más antiguas que se muestran arriba son _____ .

7. Los reptiles aparecieron durante la misma era que los helechos, peces y _____ .

8. Gusanos y aguamalas aparecieron primero en el tiempo _____..

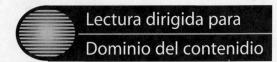

Lectura dirigida para Dominio del contenidio

Sección 1 ▪ **La vida y el tiempo geológico**
Sección 2 ▪ **Historia temprana de la Tierra**

Instrucciones: *Encierra en un círculo el término en paréntesis que completa correctamente cada oración.*

1. La subdivisión más grande del tiempo geológico es el(la) (época, eon).

2. La división de la historia de la Tierra en unidades de tiempo conforma la (escala del tiempo geológico, escala del tiempo trilobíteca).

3. Un grupo de organismos que sólo se reproduce con miembros de su grupo es una (población, especie).

4. El proceso por medio del cual los organismos que se adaptan bien a su ambiente sobreviven y se reproducen se llama (selección natural, evolución orgánica).

5. Pangaea se formó durante la era (Paleozoica, Mesozoica).

6. Una subdivisión de las eras llamada (épocas, períodos), se caracteriza por los tipos de organismos que existían a nivel mundial.

7. Los(as) (fósiles, placas) ayudan a los científicos a dividir la historia de la Tierra en unidades de tiempo.

8. El cambio de los organismos a lo largo del tiempo geológico se conoce como (selección natural, evolución orgánica).

9. Las rocas más antiguas de la Tierra (no) contienen (solo unos cuantos) fósiles.

10. La Era Precámbrica es la parte (más larga, más corta) de la historia de la Tierra.

11. Las cianobacterias son bacterias (incoloras, azul verdosas) que se cree fueron una de las primeras formas de vida de la Tierra.

Instrucciones: *Escribe A, B, C, D o E bajo la ilustración apropiada para mostrar el orden en que aparecieron los organismos sobre la Tierra.*

Reptile   Cianobacterias   Peces   Anfibio   Aguamalas

 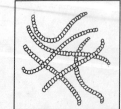 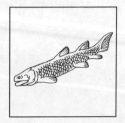  

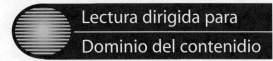

Lectura dirigida para
Dominio del contenidio

Sección 3 ▪ Historia media y reciente de la Tierra

Instrucciones: *Usa los siguientes términos para rellenar la tabla.*

aves	hace 65 millones de años	*Homo sapiens*	Pangaea
Alpes e Himalayas	dinosaurios	angiospermas	

E r a	Lapso de tiempo	Período	Formas de vida	Evento geológico
Mesozoica	245 a 65 millones de años antes del presente	Triásico	Aparecieron los primeros 2. _____ pequeños.	Todos los continentes estaban unidos en una sola masa llamada 6. _____.
		Jurásico	Apareció el(la) primer(a) 3. _____.	
		Cretáceo	Evolucionaron nuevas plantas llamadas 4. _____	
Cenozoica	1. _____ _____ al presente.	Terciario	Se extinguieron los dinosaurios.	Comienzan a elevarse 7. _____ Comienza la glaciación.
		Cuarternario	Apareció 5. _____ *sapiens*.	

Instrucciones: *Para cada uno de los siguientes, escribe la letra del término o frase que complete mejor cada oración.*

_____ **8.** La Era Mesozoica también se conoce como la era de _____.
    a. vida intermedia   **b.** vida nueva

_____ **9.** Las aves aparecieron durante el Período _____.
    a. Triásico   **b.** Jurásico

Satisface las necesidades individuales

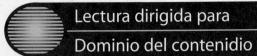

Lectura dirigida para Dominio del contenidio

Palabras claves
El tiempo geológico

Instrucciones: *Conecta con una línea cada descripción a la izquierda con el término correcto a la derecha.*

1. subdivisiones grandes del tiempo geológico basadas en las diferencias en los seres vivos

2. organismos que vivieron hace cientos de millones de años y que tenían el cuerpo dividido en tres secciones

3. la parte geológica más larga de la historia de la Tierra

4. una de las formas vivientes más tempranas, la cual producían oxígeno

5. animales voladores que evolucionaron a partir de los dinosaurios

6. masa de tierra única que una vez incluyó a todos los continentes

7. unidad más corta en un período geológico

8. período de tiempo durante el cual los dinosaurios eran la forma de vida dominante

9. división de la historia de la Tierra en unidades de tiempo

10. las subdivisiones más largas tiempo geológico

11. principales divisiones de una era

12. cambio en los organismos a lo largo del tiempo

13. grupo de organismos que normalmente sólo se reproduce con miembros del mismo grupo

14. proceso por medio del cual sólo ciertos organismos sobreviven y se reproducen

Precámbrico

escala del tiempo geológico

eras

especies

trilobites

períodos

Pangaea

selección natural

cianobacterias

eones

aves

evolución orgánica

Jurásico

época

Life and Geologic Time

Directions: *Answer the following questions on the lines provided.*

1. What determines the divisions of eras and periods on the geologic time scale?

_____

2. Which of the eras on the geologic time scale is divided into both periods and epochs?

_____

3. Why do scientists study fossils? _____

_____

4. How do trilobite eyes indicate the environment they lived in?

_____

_____

5. Why are trilobites considered index fossils?

_____

_____

6. What factors in the environment or surroundings would cause a species to change?

_____

_____

7. How might geologic events, such as the movement of tectonic plates, affect the environment in which species live?

_____

_____

8. Why did some ancient fish have lungs as well as gills?

_____

_____

9. In what sort of environment must amphibians lay their eggs?

_____

_____

10. In what epoch, period, and era do you live?

_____

_____

Meeting Individual Needs

Early Earth History

Directions: *List the events and types of organisms below in the order in which they happened or appeared on Earth. The oldest one is Number 1.*

amphibians   complex organisms   cyanobacteria   fish   invertebrates

organisms with hard parts   shielding of Earth from ultraviolet rays

Pangaea   reptiles   oxygen is major atmospheric gas

1. _____

2. _____

3. _____

4. _____

5. _____

6. _____

7. _____

8. _____

9. _____

10. _____

Directions: *Answer the following questions on the lines provided.*

11. Which of the events in your list above occurred in the Precambrian time? Which occurred in

the Paleozoic Era? _____

_____

12. Why is so little known about the Precambrian time? _____

_____

_____

13. Where did most life-forms of the Paleozoic Era live? _____

_____

_____

14. What might have caused the mass extinctions at the end of the Paleozoic Era?

_____

_____

_____

Middle and Recent Earth History

Directions: *Match the descriptions in Column I with the terms in Column II. Write the letter of the correct term in the space provided in the left-hand column.*

Column I

_____ 1. seed plants which first appeared in the Paleozoic Era

_____ 2. era of "middle life"

_____ 3. most recent period in the Mesozoic Era

_____ 4. oldest period in the Mesozoic Era

_____ 5. northern part of Pangaea

_____ 6. southern part of Pangaea

_____ 7. fast-moving dinosaur

_____ 8. dinosaur thought to nurture hatchlings

_____ 9. winged animal resembling both dinosaurs and birds

_____ 10. milk-producing animals; first appeared in the Triassic Period

_____ 11. flowering plants

_____ 12. most recent era

_____ 13. most recent period in the Cenozoic Era

_____ 14. climate change that allowed flowering plants to increase

_____ 15. where most marsupials live

_____ 16. animals with pouches

Column II

a. Gondwanaland

b. mammals

c. Australia

d. Laurasia

e. Cretaceous

f. gymnosperms

g. angiosperms

h. Mesozoic

i. Quaternary

j. *Maiasaura*

k. Triassic

l. Cenozoic

m. marsupials

n. tyrannosaurs

o. cooling

p. *Archaeopteryx*

q. *Gallimimus*

Meeting Individual Needs

Directions: *Complete the following statements.*

17. The bones of cold-blooded animals have _____.

18. The bones of dinosaurs resemble those of _____-blooded animals.

19. Some dinosaurs may have _____ their young.

SECTION 1 Enrichment

The Earliest Primates

Fossils have allowed scientists to trace the evolution of not just trilobites, but of many species of animals. From the fossils, scientists have learned a tremendous amount about what earlier forms of these animals looked like. One of the problems, though, in studying fossils is that often not all of the fossil skeleton can be found. Therefore, scientists have to draw conclusions about the animal without being able to see and study the animal's entire structure. This particular problem led to some interesting "reconclusions" about primates in 1990.

Primates

Primates are a group of about 200 species of animals that include lemurs, monkeys, apes, and humans. They are grouped together on the basis of similar skeletal and other features. It's believed that they have a common ancestor and developed into separate species over millions of years.

For a long time, paleontologists thought that the oldest primates were the 60-million-year-old creatures they named plesiadapiforms. Plesiadapiform fossils included teeth, jaws, and parts of skulls. From the fossils, scientists concluded that plesiadapiform was a primate. Certainly, its teeth were like those of other primates. They were adapted for grinding, designed for a diet of insects, fruits, and seeds.

Is it a primate?

In 1990, new plesiadapiform bones were dug up in Wyoming. These included the first complete skull and some fingers and wrists which were parts that had never been found before. The paleontologists who studied the finger bones were surprised to find that they did not resemble those of primates. The only living animal with a similar arrangement of finger bones is a small, tree-dwelling mammal of the Borneo and Philippine rain forests, called a colugo. The scientists who examined the intact skull identified it as resembling that of the colugo. The conclusion was the plesiadapiforms were not primates, since colugos are not primates.

Other scientists were studying an animal discovered at the foot of the High Atlas Mountains in Morocco. The creature, called the *Altiatlasius*, lived 60 million years ago. The paleontologists found ten tiny teeth similar to those in one of today's smallest primates, the 57-gram mouse lemur of Madagascar.

The earliest primate?

Another animal, less advanced but much larger than the *Altiatlasius*, has also been found. Many scientists are calling it an earlier primate. It's a house-cat-sized microsyopid and may have lived more than 60 million years ago. It's identified as an early primate from its bone structure.

1. If the microsyopid is proved to be a primate, what conclusion about primates might be changed?

_____

_____

2. Why do you think the *Altiatlasius* was so named?

_____

_____

3. What does the reading tell you about scientific inquiries?

_____

_____

Meeting Individual Needs

SECTION 2 Enrichment

Extinction and Paleozoic Life

When the birth rate of a species is lower than its death rate for a prolonged period of time, extinction might occur. Extinction means that a species dies out forever. Scientists believe extinction occurs because the species is not able to adapt to a changing environment. For example, if a certain kind of fish lives in fresh water but for some reason the water becomes brackish, or part saltwater, then the species of fish will either adapt or die out completely. Scientists say that of all the species that have ever lived, more than 99 percent are extinct.

Background Extinction

Most extinctions occur over a period of time. This is called *background extinction*. Scientists say that as many as 95 percent of extinctions are background extinctions. There are many causes of background extinction including small changes in climate or habitat, competition or war between species, and depletion or using up of resources needed by the species.

Mass Extinction

Another thing that can happen is a mass extinction. A mass extinction is a sudden, worldwide decrease in species. There have been five mass extinctions in the history of the world. For an extinction to be considered a mass extinction, it must:

- be global
- impact a number of species
- take place within a relatively short period of time

During the Paleozoic Era, there were six distinct periods of time: Cambrian, Ordovician, Silurian, Devonian, Carboniferous, and Permian. During the Ordovician period of time, a mass extinction occurred. Scientists say it is the second largest mass extinction in history. More than 100 families of marine invertebrates disappeared during the extinction.

Meeting Individual Needs

Directions: *Use resources from the library to help you answer the following questions.*

1. Which kinds of animals lived during the six time periods of the Paleozoic Era?

_____

_____

_____

2. Besides the Ordovician Mass Extinction, were there any other mass extinctions during the Paleozoic Era?

_____

_____

3. Did any Paleozoic Era animal life survive? Explain.

_____

_____

_____

4. Why do you think most extinctions occur as background extinctions?

_____

_____

Autumn Leaves

It's remarkable to find 17 million-year-old fossil leaves. It's more remarkable to find 17 million-year-old leaves themselves. But such leaves have been found. According to the scientist who reported this discovery, Edward Golenberg, about 17 million years ago a storm tore autumn leaves from trees growing near a lake in what is now northern Idaho. The leaves, some green and some red, settled into the cold, oxygen-free sediment at the bottom of the lake. The absence of oxygen keeps bacteria from growing and causing plants to decay. The leaves were quickly covered with mud. Over time, the lake dried up. The mud turned to rock, and the leaves were sealed away from destruction for millions of years.

Studying the Leaves

Golenberg found that the rock-encased leaves immediately fell apart when the rocks were broken. But he was able to save some parts by placing them in a solution. This allowed scientists to study the genetic material that made up these ancient plants. The appearance of the leaves indicated that they were an extinct species of magnolia. Examination of the genetic material supported this theory.

Ancient Magnolias

This ancient magnolia, like the magnolias of today, is an angiosperm. The seeds of angiosperms are enclosed in a seed case. Insects and birds and sometimes wind carry angiosperm pollen from flower to flower to fertilize the plants. After fertilization, the flowers close and the developing seeds are protected. Gymnosperms, the other kind of seed-producing plant, produce seeds with no seed case. Conifers such as pine and fir trees are typical gymnosperms. The flowers of gymnosperms are barely noticeable, and gymnosperms depend on wind and gravity for pollination.

Which came first?

Although some scientists believe that angiosperms evolved from gymnosperms, the question of when and how angiosperms like the ancient magnolias first appeared is still a mystery. To date, no magnolia-like flower fossils have been found.

1. How does Golenberg's discovery differ from most discoveries that reveal information about

   ancient plants? _____

   _____

2. Explain how the leaves remained intact, rather than being decomposed, at the bottom of

   the lake. _____

   _____

3. Do you think trees in autumn looked very different 17 million years ago than they do today?

   Explain. _____

   _____

   _____

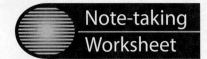

Geologic Time

Note-taking Worksheet

Section 1   Life and Geologic Time

A. _____ time—Earth's history is divided into time units that make up a

geologic time scale.

1. Time units on the scale are based on the appearance or disappearance of types of organisms

such as _____, index fossils that lived during specific periods of time.

2. Geologic time is divided into four major _____.

   a. _____—longest subdivision; based on abundance of fossils

   b. _____—marked by significant worldwide changes in the types of fossils

   present in rock

   c. _____—based on types of life existing worldwide at a particular time

   d. _____—characterized by differences in life-forms, but differences can be

   regional rather than global

3. Geologic time can be subdivided only if fossils are present in rock records.

B. _____ **evolution**—Organisms have changed over time, most likely because of

environmental changes.

1. **Species**—organisms that normally _____ only with other members of

   their group

2. Darwin's theory of **natural** _____—organisms more adapted to an

   environment are more likely to reproduce

3. Natural selection within a species occurs only if characteristics present in some numbers

   increase their _____.

4. _____ selection—breeding individuals with desired characteristics;

   humans use this type of selection when breeding domestic animals

5. _____ species can evolve from natural selection.

C. Trilobites—have an exoskeleton with three lobes; lived in oceans for more than 200 million years

1. Trilobite _____ position changed as the species adapted to various environments.

2. Trilobite bodies and _____ changed in response to changing environments.

Meeting Individual Needs

Note-taking Worksheet (continued)

3. Continental collisions formed the giant landmass _____ near the end of the Paleozoic _____. These collisions may have dropped _____, causing the extinction of trilobites.

Section 2   Early Earth History

A. _____ time—from 4 billion to about 544 million years ago

1. Very few _____ remain from this time.

    a. Many Precambrian rocks were deeply buried, causing the fossils in them to be changed by _____ and pressure.

    b. Most Precambrian organisms lacked _____ parts.

2. **Cyanobacteria** are blue-green _____.

    a. One of the _____ life forms to appear

    b. Added _____ to the atmosphere through photosynthesis

3. _____ and Ediacaran animals appeared late in Precambrian time.

B. The _____ Era—about 544 million years ago to about 245 million years ago

1. Many organisms with _____ and vertebrates evolved in the warm, shallow seas.

2. _____ evolved to survive in water and on land.

    a. Might have evolved from _____

    b. Could obtain oxygen from _____ or from lungs.

3. _____ evolved from amphibians to survive farther from water

4. Several mountain-building episodes occurred during the Paleozoic Era because of _____ collisions.

5. Most marine and land species became _____ at the end of the Paleozoic Era.

Section 3   Middle and Recent Earth History

A. _____ Era—lasted from 245 to 65 million years ago

1. Pangaea separated into _____ and the climate became drier.

2. _____ evolved; they might have been warm-blooded, traveled in herds, and nurtured their young.

Note-taking Worksheet (continued)

3. _____, which probably evolved from small, meat-eating dinosaurs, appeared during the Jurassic Period.

4. Small, mouse-like _____, which are warm-blooded vertebrates with hair and milk to feed their young, appeared in the Triassic Period.

5. _____, plants that produce seeds but not flowers, appeared in the Paleozoic Era.

6. Flowering plants or _____ appeared during the Cretaceous Period.

7. A great extinction, perhaps caused by a comet or an asteroid collision, occurred about _____ years ago, marking the end of the Mesozoic Era.

B. The _____ **Era** began about 65 million years ago and continues today.

1. Many _____ formed, perhaps creating cooler climates worldwide.

2. Mammals continued to evolve

   a. Many species became _____ as the continents continued to separate.

   b. *Homo sapiens,* or _____, appeared about 400,000 years ago.

Assessment

Chapter Review

Geologic Time

Part A. Vocabulary Review

Directions: Write the terms in the blanks at the left of their descriptions and then circle the 11 terms in the puzzle .

_____ 1. animals evolved from a species of amphibians

_____ 2. animals that live on land but return to water to reproduce

_____ 3. animals without a backbone

_____ 4. division of Earth's history into smaller units

_____ 5. among the earliest life-forms on Earth

_____ 6. group of organisms that normally reproduce only among themselves

_____ 7. animals with a backbone

_____ 8. flowering plants

_____ 9. naked seed plants

_____ 10. organism used to identify specific geologic time period

_____ 11. process by which organisms with traits that are suited to a certain environment survive whereas others do not

```
G E O L O G I C T I M E S C A L E V B
K D C Z B A J Y Q R E P T I L E S D M
V F M D K L T A M P H I B I A N S X I
T X K O R Y A N O C E P O L L T M O N
B X D G Y M N O S P E R M S R X D R D
I N V E R T E B R A T E S S Z J C K E
M B Y F M Y R A N G I O S P E R M S X
X D F L V P P C Q J D J Q E K Z M L F
C H X B I B A T K S A R D C F T K V O
J Y K D Q D V E V C F K F I Q B J C S
M V E R T E B R A T E S B E R A R T S
B K A B K X Z I P R B Z T S C S Z K I
A Z N A T U R A L S E L E C T I O N L
```

Assessment

Chapter Review (continued)

Part B. Concept Review

Directions: *Answer the following questions on the lines provided.*

1. What units divide the geologic time scale?

   _____

   _____

2. Describe the life-forms of Precambrian time.

   _____

   _____

   _____

   _____

3. What evolutionary change in life-forms marked the beginning of the Paleozoic Era, and what event marked the end of the era? What life-forms dominated the era?

   _____

   _____

   _____

4. How did plate tectonics affect the evolution of life in the Mesozoic Era?

   _____

   _____

   _____

   _____

5. During which epoch did humans probably appear?

   _____

   _____

6. What events occurred that allowed single-celled organisms to evolve into more complex organisms at the end of the Precambrian time?

   _____

   _____

   _____

Geologic Time

Chapter Test

I. Testing Concepts

Directions: *Write the letter of the term or phrase that correctly completes the statement or answers the question.*

_____ 1. Geologic time is divided into units based on _____.
    a. geologic changes
    b. fossils and rocks
    c. types of life-forms living during certain periods
    d. all of these

_____ 2. Humans appeared in the _____ Era.
    a. Cenozoic
    b. Paleozoic
    c. Mesozoic
    d. Devonian

_____ 3. The major divisions in geologic time are _____.
    a. epochs
    b. periods
    c. centuries
    d. eons

_____ 4. Changes in the exoskeleton of trilobites probably occurred because of _____.
    a. geographic isolation
    b. changing environments
    c. the competition for survival
    d. all of these

_____ 5. Species of _____ existed during the Mesozoic Era.
    a. birds
    b. mammals
    c. both a and b
    d. neither a nor b

_____ 6. Life-forms that first appeared in the Cenozoic Era include _____.
    a. humans
    b. reptiles
    c. mammals
    d. all of these

_____ 7. The development of ozone in the stratosphere and oxygen in the atmosphere first made possible the development of _____.
    a. complex organisms
    b. single-cell organisms
    c. cyanobacteria
    d. all of these

_____ 8. Today, many scientists think that _____.
    a. birds evolved from dinosaurs
    b. dinosaurs evolved from reptiles
    c. birds evolved from amphibians
    d. both a and b

_____ 9. Ediacaran organisms first appeared during the _____.
    a. Precambrian Time
    b. Cambrian Period
    c. Permian Period
    d. none of these

_____ 10. As _____ evolved, they changed Earth's atmosphere by producing oxygen.
    a. cyanobacteria
    b. trilobites
    c. reptiles
    d. dinosaurs

Assessment

_____ 11. A life-form that evolved during the Paleozoic Era was _____.
    a. cyanobacteria   c. reptiles
    b. humans   d. dinosaurs

_____ 12. The end of the Paleozoic Era might have involved _____.
    a. the development of humans
    b. mass extinctions of land and sea animals
    c. the appearance of marine animals with hard parts
    d. both a and b

_____ 13. A life-form that evolved during the Mesozoic Era was the _____.
    a. human   c. reptile
    b. dinosaur   d. cyanobacteria

_____ 14. Large mammals of the Cenozoic Era may have become extinct because of activity by _____.
    a. volcanoes   c. plate tectonics
    b. humans   d. all of these

_____ 15. Trilobites can be used to study the passage of geologic time because _____.
    a. they burrowed into sediments
    b. they lived in the oceans
    c. they lived throughout the Paleozoic Era
    d. their physical features changed through time

_____ 16. A trilobite with no eyes was best adapted for life _____.
    a. on land   c. near the water's surface
    b. as an active swimmer   d. deeper than light could penetrate

_____ 17. Plate tectonics may affect changes in species because movement of plates causes a change in _____.
    a. Earth's surface   c. the environment
    b. climates   d. all of these

_____ 18. Plate tectonics during the Mesozoic Era caused _____.
    a. Pangaea to separate   c. human life to form
    b. Pangaea to form   d. dinosaurs to become extinct

II. Understanding Concepts

Skill: Recognizing Cause and Effect

Directions: *Answer the following questions on the lines provided.*

1. What effect does plate tectonics have on evolution of new species? _____

_____

2. How did plate tectonics affect the evolution of dominant animal life during the Mesozoic Era?

_____

_____

Assessment

Chapter Test (continued)

3. What is one effect of increased human activity in the Cenozoic Era on habitats of some species?

_____

_____

4. What trait has made angiosperms the dominant land plant today?

_____

_____

Skill: Sequencing Events

Directions: *List the events below in correct sequence according to the geologic time scale. List the oldest event as 5 and the most recent as 9.*

<table>
<tr><td>development of birds</td><td>dinosaurs as dominant life-form</td></tr>
<tr><td>appearance of humans</td><td>evolution of cyanobacteria</td></tr>
<tr><td colspan="2">disappearance of Ediacaran fauna</td></tr>
</table>

5. _____

6. _____

7. _____

8. _____

9. _____

Skill: Making a Table

Directions: *Fill in the table showing the Cenozoic Era on the geologic time scale. Include periods, epochs, and information about species.*

10.

Cenozoic Era

Period	Epochs	Species

Chapter Test (continued)

III. Applying Concepts

Writing Skills

Directions: *Answer the following questions in complete sentences on the lines provided.*

1. How does plate tectonics affect development of new species?

_____

_____

2. Why is little known about 90 percent of Earth's history?

_____

_____

3. Why were reptiles able to develop from amphibians?

_____

_____

4. Describe some of the changes in the land and its life-forms that occurred at the end of the Paleozoic Era.

_____

_____

5. Why couldn't complex organisms develop before the establishment of an ozone layer?

_____

_____

6. Why do trilobites make excellent index fossils?

_____

_____

7. What is the most significant difference between Precambrian and Paleozoic life-forms?

_____

_____

8. Explain why modern birds are related to the Archaeopteryx even though not descended from it.

_____

_____

9. Contrast the animal life of the Mesozoic Era with that of the early Cenozoic Era.

_____

_____

Transparency
Activities

SECTION 1 — Section Focus Transparency Activity

Relatively Speaking . . .

The spectacular bands of multicolored rock at sites like the Vermillion Cliffs are more than just beautiful. They are tools that help us learn about the history of Earth. As you examine the contours of this canyon, think about what these layers tell us.

1. Do you think all the rock in the picture was formed at the same time? Why or why not?

2. If you think the rock formed at different times, which layers are the oldest and which are the youngest?

3. If you were comparing two different fossils, what information might be revealed if you knew their location within the rock layers?

Transparency Activities

SECTION 2 Section Focus Transparency Activity

An Early Plant

This is a fossil of *Cooksonia,* one of the earliest land plants known to scientists. These fossils are about 420 million years old—that's about 200 million years before the dinosaurs lived!

1. What characteristics of *Cooksonia* are similar to plants that you see every day?

2. Would you guess that plants or animals colonized land first?

Transparency Activities

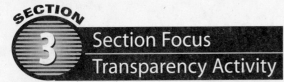

SECTION 3 Section Focus
Transparency Activity

Big Smile for the Camera

The oldest fossils of sharks date back nearly 400 million years. The ancestors of modern sharks, though, first appeared about 200 million years ago. Below is a great white shark, a creature that hasn't changed much since its family arose during the Jurassic Period. Since that time, the swimming mechanisms of sharks have improved, and so have their feeding abilities.

1. What animals were dominant on land as sharks arose in the oceans?

2. Why are sharks sometimes called living fossils?

3. Can you name any other animals that have survived for such a long time with little change?

Transparency Activities

Geologic Time Scale

			Millions of years ago
Cenozoic Era	Quaternary Period	Holocene Epoch	
			0.008
		Pleistocene Epoch	
			1.8
	Tertiary Period	Pliocene Epoch	
			5.3 ← Himalaya rise
		Miocene Epoch	
			23.8
		Oligocene Epoch	
			33.7
		Eocene Epoch	
			55.5
		Paleocene Epoch	
			65 ← Mass extinction
Mesozoic Era	Cretaceous Period		← First flowering plants
			145
	Jurassic Period		← First birds
			213
	Triassic Period		← Pangaea breaks apart
			248 ← Mass extinction
Paleozoic Era	Permian Period		
			286
	Pennsylvanian Period		← First reptiles
			325
	Mississippian Period		
			360
	Devonian Period		← First amphibians
			410
	Silurian Period		← First land plants
			440
	Ordovician Period		← First fish
			505
	Cambrian Period		← First trilobites
			544
Precambrian Time	Proterozoic Eon		
			2,500
	Archaean Eon		← First life
			3,800
	Hadean Eon		
			4,500 ← Origin of Earth

Teaching Transparency Activity (continued)

1. Arrange the following terms in order of the length of time they represent. Place the longest time interval first: *period, era, epoch.*

_____

2. Why is the fossil record from Precambrian time so sparse?

_____

_____

_____

3. About how many years separate the beginning of the Devonian Period from the beginning of the Pennsylvanian Period? Which period is more recent?

_____

_____

4. During what era and period did the first amphibians appear?

_____

5. Would researchers be amazed to find a 400-million-year-old fossil of a fish? Why or why not?

_____

_____

6. Would researchers think it unusual to find a bird fossil that dated back to the Permian Period? Why or why not?

_____

_____

 **Geologic Time**

Directions: *Carefully review the table and answer the following questions.*

Geologic Time Scale		
Era	**When was it?**	**Types of species that appeared**
Cenozoic	65 million years ago to today	Humans, larger mammals
Mesozoic	248–65 million years ago	Small mammals, birds, dinosaurs, angiosperms
Paleozoic	544–248 million years ago	Early reptiles, amphibians, fish, gymnosperms
Precambrian	4.5 billion years to 545 million years ago	Worms, jellyfish

1. According to the table, a fossil of a dinosaur would probably be from the ___.
   A Cenozoic Era
   B Mesozoic Era
   C Paleozoic Era
   D Precambrian Era

2. According to the table, which geologic period occurred more than 800 million years ago?
   F Cenozoic Era
   G Mesozoic Era
   H Paleozoic Era
   J Precambrian Era

3. According to the table, early ancestors of frogs would have appeared during the ___.
   A Cenozoic Era
   B Mesozoic Era
   C Paleozoic Era
   D Precambrian Era

Transparency Activities

Expanded Geologic Time Scale

Homo sapiens evolves; most recent ice ages occur; Grand Canyon forms.

Cenozoic Era

Quaternary Period
1.6 M.Y.B.P.
Holocene Epoch   0.008 M.Y.B.P.
Pleistocene Epoch   1.8 M.Y.B.P.

Neogene Period
23 M.Y.B.P.
Pliocene Epoch   5.3 M.Y.B.P.
Miocene Epoch   23.8 M.Y.B.P.

Paleogene Period
65 M.Y.B.P.
Oligocene Epoch   37.7 M.Y.B.P.
Eocene Epoch   55.5 M.Y.B.P.
Paleocene Epoch   65 M.Y.B.P.

Mammals are abundant; angiosperms are dominant; Alps and the Himalayas begin to rise.

Dinsaurs become extinct.

Dinosaurs are dominant; first birds appear; mountain building continues in western North America.

Mesozoic Era

Cretaceous Peroid
145 M.Y.B.P.

Jurassic Period
213 M.Y.B.P.

Triassic Period
248 M.Y.B.P.

Angiosperms appear; Rocky Mountains begin to form.

First mammals and cycads appear; Atlantic Ocean begins to form, Pangaea breaks up.

Many marine invertebrates become extinct; building of Appalachians ends; glaciers retreat.

Paleozoic Era

Permian Period
286 M.Y.B.P.

Pennsylvanian Period
325 M.Y.B.P.

Mississippian Period
360 M.Y.B.P.

Devonian Period
410 M.Y.B.P.

Silurian Period
440 M.Y.B.P.

Ordovician Period
505 M.Y.B.P.

Cambrian Period
544 M.Y.B.P.

Reptiles evolve; coal swamps form; shallow seas begin to withdraw.

Fish are dominant; first amphibians appear; Appalachians continue to form in North America and Europe.

First land plants form; first insects evolve.

First fish appear; Appalachians begin to form.

Amphibians are dominant; glacial advances occur.

Corals and other invertebrates are dominant; warm, shallow seas cover much of North America.

Trilobites, brachiopods, other marine invertebrates are abundant; thick sediments deposited in inland seas.

Precambrian Time

Ediacaran organisms develop.

Bacteria-like organisms form; microfossils appear; several episodes of mountain building occur.

4600 M.Y.B.P.*

*Millions of years before present that each unit of time began

Teacher Support and Planning

Content Outline for Teaching

Geologic Time

Section 1 Life and Geologic Time

A. <u>Geologic</u> time—Earth's history is divided into time units that make up a **geologic time scale**.

   1. Time units on the scale are based on the appearance or disappearance of types of organisms such as **trilobites**, index fossils that lived during specific periods of time.

   2. Geologic time is divided into four major <u>subdivisions</u>.

      a. <u>Eons</u>—longest subdivision; based on abundance of fossils

      b. <u>Eras</u>—marked by significant worldwide changes in the types of fossils present in rock

      c. <u>Periods</u>—based on types of life existing worldwide at a particular time

      d. <u>Epochs</u>—characterized by differences in life-forms, but differences can be regional rather than global

   3. Geologic time can be subdivided only if fossils are present in rock records.

B. <u>Organic evolution</u>—Organisms have changed over time, most likely because of environmental changes.

   1. **Species**—organisms that normally <u>reproduce</u> only with other members of their group

   2. Darwin's theory of **natural <u>selection</u>**—organisms more adapted to an environment are more likely to reproduce

   3. Natural selection within a species occurs only if characteristics present in some numbers increase their <u>survival</u>.

   4. <u>Artificial</u> selection—breeding individuals with desired characteristics; humans use this type of selection when breeding domestic animals.

   5. <u>New</u> species can evolve from natural selection.

C. Trilobites—have an exoskeleton with three lobes; lived in oceans for more than 200 million years

   1. Trilobite <u>eye</u> position changed as the species adapted to various environments.

   2. Trilobite bodies and <u>tails</u> changed in response to changing environments.

   3. Continental collisions formed the giant landmass **Pangaea** near the end of the Paleozoic <u>Era</u>. These collisions may have dropped <u>sea levels</u>, causing the extinction of trilobites.

DISCUSSION QUESTION:

What is a species? *A group of organisms that normally reproduce only with each other*

Section 2   Early Earth History

A. <u>Precambrian</u> time—from 4 billion to about 544 million years ago

   1. Very few <u>fossils</u> remain from this time.

      a. Many Precambrian rocks were deeply buried, causing the fossils in them to be changed by <u>heat</u> and pressure.

      b. Most Precambrian organisms lacked <u>hard</u> parts.

   2. **Cyanobacteria** are blue-green <u>algae</u>.

      a. One of the <u>earliest</u> life forms to appear

      b. Added <u>oxygen</u> to the atmosphere through photosynthesis

   3. <u>Invertebrates</u> and Ediacaran animals appeared late in Precambrian time.

B. The <u>Paleozoic</u> Era—about 544 million years ago to about 245 million years ago

   1. Many organisms with <u>shells</u> and vertebrates evolved in the warm, shallow seas.

   2. <u>Amphibians</u> evolved to survive in water and on land.

      a. Might have evolved from <u>fish</u>

      b. Could obtain oxygen from <u>gills</u> or from lungs.

   3. <u>Reptiles</u> evolved from amphibians to survive farther from water.

   4. Several mountain-building episodes occurred during the Paleozoic Era because of <u>plate</u> collisions.

   5. Most marine and land species became <u>extinct</u> at the end of the Paleozoic Era.

DISCUSSION QUESTION:

How did cyanobacteria affect the atmosphere? *They produced oxygen through photosynthesis, which made oxygen a major atmospheric gas for the few billion years following their appearance.*

Content Outline for Teaching (continued)

Section 3   Middle and Recent Earth History

A. <u>Mesozoic</u> Era—lasted from 245 to 65 million years ago

   1. Pangaea separated into <u>continents</u> and the climate became drier.

   2. <u>Dinosaurs</u> evolved; they might have been warm-blooded, traveled in herds, and nurtured their young.

   3. <u>Birds</u>, which probably evolved from small, meat-eating dinosaurs, appeared during the Jurassic Period.

   4. Small, mouse-like <u>mammals</u>, which are warm-blooded vertebrates with hair and milk to feed their young, appeared in the Triassic Period.

   5. <u>Gymnosperms</u>, plants that produce seeds but not flowers, appeared in the Paleozoic Era.

   6. Flowering plants or <u>angiosperms</u> appeared during the Cretaceous Period.

   7. A great extinction, perhaps caused by a comet or an asteroid collision, occurred about <u>65 million</u> years ago, marking the end of the Mesozoic Era.

B. The **<u>Cenozoic</u> Era** began about 65 million years ago and continues today.

   1. Many <u>mountain ranges</u> formed, perhaps creating cooler climates worldwide.

   2. Mammals continued to evolve

      a. Many species became <u>isolated</u> as the continents continued to separate.

      b. *Homo sapiens*, or <u>humans</u>, appeared about 400,000 years ago.

DISCUSSION QUESTION:

What were the first mammals like and when did they appear? *They were small, mouse-like mammals. They appeared in the Triassic Period.*

El tiempo geológico

SECCIÓN 1 La vida y el tiempo geológico

Lo que aprenderás

- A explicar la división del tiempo geológico en unidades.
- A relacionar los cambios en los organismos de la Tierra con las divisiones de la escala del tiempo geológico.
- A describir el efecto de la tectónica de placas sobre las especies.

Vocabulario

trilobite / trilobites: organismo con un exoesqueleto dividido en tres partes; existía en abundancia en los océanos del Paleozoico; se le considera un fósil guía.

geologic time scale / escala del tiempo geológico: división de la historia de la Tierra en unidades cronológicas que se basan en gran parte en los tipos de formas de vida que existieron solamente durante ciertos períodos.

eon / eón: la subdivisión más larga de la escala del tiempo geológico, basada en la abundancia de ciertos tipos de fósiles; se subdivide en eras, períodos y épocas.

era / era: segunda división mayor del tiempo geológico; se subdivide en períodos y se basa en cambios importantes a nivel mundial en los tipos de fósiles.

period / período: hilera horizontal de elementos en la tabla periódica cuyas propiedades cambian paulatinamente y son predecibles.

epoch / época: la siguiente subdivisión de tiempo geológico que le sigue al período; se caracteriza por diferencias en formas de vida que pueden variar regionalmente.

organic evolution / evolución orgánica: cambio de organismos a través del tiempo geológico.

species / especie: grupo de organismos que se reproduce sólo con otros miembros de su propio grupo.

natural selection / selección natural: proceso por el cual los organismos que están adaptados a un entorno en particular son más capaces de sobrevivir y reproducirse que organismos que no lo están.

Pangaea / Pangaea: masa de tierra extensa y antigua que una vez estuvo formada por todos los continentes.

Por qué es importante

La vida y el paisaje a tu alrededor son el producto de los cambios a lo largo del tiempo geológico.

SECCIÓN 2 Historia temprana de la Tierra

Lo que aprenderás

- A identificar características de las formas de vida del Precámbrico y del Paleozoico.
- A sacar conclusiones acerca de cómo se adaptaron los organismos a los cambios en los ambientes de la Era Precámbrica y la Era Paleozoica.
- A describir cambios en la Tierra y en sus formas de vida a fines de la Era Paleozoica.

Vocabulario

Precambrian time / Era Precámbrica: la parte más larga de la historia de la Tierra, la cual duró de 4.0 billones hasta hace cerca de 544 millones de años.

cyanobacteria / cianobacterias: bacterias fotosintéticas que contienen clorofila y que se piensa son unas de las primeras formas de vida terrestre.

Paleozoic Era / Era Paleozoica: era de vida antigua, la cual comenzó hace unos 544 millones de años, cuando los organismos desarrollaron partes duras y terminó con extinciones en masa hace unos 245 millones de años.

Por qué es importante

El Precámbrico incluye la mayor parte de la historia de la Tierra.

Especies cambiantes

En esta actividad observarás cómo la adaptación dentro de una especie puede causar la evolución de un rasgo en particular, lo que puede conducir al desarrollo de una nueva especie.

Lo que investigarás

¿De qué forma puede la adaptación dentro de una especie causar la evolución de un rasgo en particular?

Materiales

Juego de cartas

Metas

- Modelar la adaptación dentro de una especie.

Procedimiento

1. Elimina todos los reyes, reinas, sotas y ases del juego de cartas.
2. Cada carta restante representa un individuo de una población de animales llamados "varimales." El número de cada carta representa la estatura del individuo. Por ejemplo, el número 5 de diamantes es un varimal de 5 unidades de estatura.
3. Calcula la estatura promedio de la población de varimales representada por tus cartas.
4. Supón que los varimales comen pasto, arbustos y hojas de los árboles. Una sequía hace que muchas de estas plantas mueran. Todo lo que queda son unos cuantos árboles altos. Solo los varimales de por lo menos 6 unidades de estatura pueden alcanzar las hojas de estos árboles.
5. Todos los animales de menos de 6 unidades de estatura dejan la zona, en busca de alimento en otras partes, o mueren de hambre. Elimina todas las cartas con un valor numérico de menos de 6. Calcula la nueva estatura promedio de la población de varimales.

6. Mezcla las cartas restantes.
7. Toma dos cartas cada vez. Cada par de cartas representa un par de varimales que se aparearán.
8. Las crías de cada pareja alcanzan la estatura promedio de sus padres. Calcula y anota la estatura de cada cría.
9. Repite, pero descartando todos los adultos y crías de menos de 8 unidades de estatura. Calcula ahora la nueva estatura promedio de los varimales. Incluye en este cálculo tanto los padres como las crías.

Concluye y aplica

1. ¿Cómo cambió la altura de la población?
2. Si no hubieras descartado los varimales más pequeños, ¿hubiera cambiado tanto la estatura promedio de la población? Explica.
3. ¿Por qué no se reprodujo cada miembro de la población original?
4. Si no hubiera habido varimales de más de 6 unidades de estatura en el paso 5, ¿qué le hubiera sucedido a la población?
5. Si no hubiera habido variabilidad en estatura en la población antes de que ocurriera la sequía, ¿hubiera podido la especie evolucionar hacia una especie más alta? Explica.
6. ¿De qué forma demuestra esta actividad que los rasgos de las especies evolucionan?

3 Historia media y reciente de la Tierra

Lo que aprenderás

- A comparar y contrastar formas de vida características de las eras Mesozoica y Cenozoica.
- A explicar cómo afectaron a los organismos los cambios causados por la tectónica de placas durante la Era Mesozoica.
- A identificar cuándo aparecieron por primera vez los seres humanos.

Vocabulario

Mesozoic Era / Era Mesozoica: era intermedia de la historia de la Tierra, durante la cual se separó Pangaea, aparecieron los dinosaurios y los reptiles y las gimnospermas eran las formas de vida dominantes en tierra.

Cenozoic Era / Era Cenozoica: era de vida reciente que comenzó hace 66 millones de años aproximadamente y que continúa hoy en día; incluye la primera aparición del *Homo sapiens* hace unos 400,000 años.

Por qué es importante

Muchos grupos importante de animales, como las aves y los mamíferos, aparecieron durante la Era Mesozoica.

Usa Internet Descubre el pasado

Imagina que Texas es como lo fuera hace millones de años. ¿Cuáles animales rondarían por donde estás ahora sentado? ¿Puedes imaginarte a un Tyrannosaurus rex rondando el área que es ahora el Parque Nacional de los Dinosaurios? Los animales y plantas que habitaron una vez tu región pudieron haber dejado pistas sobre su identidad: fósiles. Los científicos usan fósiles para entender cómo era la Tierra en el pasado geológico. Los fósiles pueden ayudar a determinar si un área solía ser terreno seco o si estaba bajo el agua. Los fósiles ayudan a descubrir pistas acerca de las plantas y animales que evolucionaron en el transcurso del tiempo. Para empezar a descubrir cómo ha cambiado Norte América a través del tiempo, utiliza los recursos del Internet y comparte la información con tus compañeros,

Reconoce el problema

¿Cómo ha cambiado tu región a través del tiempo geológico?

Formula una hipótesis

¿Cómo crees que era la región en la que ahora vives hace miles o millones de años? ¿Crees acaso que los tipos de plantas y animales han cambiado con el tiempo? Formula una hipótesis acerca de los cambios en los organismos y en la geografía de tu región, desde el pasado lejano hasta hoy.

Metas

- Recoger información acerca de los fósiles encontrados en tu región.
- Comunicar detalles acerca de los fósiles encontrados en tu región.
- Resumir la información sobre el registro fósil y los cambio en tu región que obtuviste de las diferentes fuentes.

Utiliza métodos científicos

Prueba tu hipótesis

Planifica

1. Determina la edad de las rocas de tu región. ¿Se formaron durante la Era Precámbrica, la Era Paleozoica, la Era Mesozoica o la Era Cenozoica?
2. Recoge información acerca de los animales y plantas fósiles que se han encontrado en tu región durante uno de los intervalos de tiempo nombrados arriba. Encuentra información específica sobre cuándo, adónde y cómo vivían los organismos fósiles. Si no se conocen fósiles de tu región, encuentra información acerca de los fósiles encontrados lo más cerca posible a tu región.

Realiza

1. Asegúrate de que tu maestro aprueba tus planes antes de comenzar.
2. Visita el sitio Web de Glencoe Science science.glencoe.com y publica tus datos en la tabla. Agrega cualquier información que crees es importante para comprender los fósiles de tu región.

Teacher Support & Planning

Analiza tus datos

1. ¿Qué animales o plantas prehistóricos tienen posibles parientes que existen hoy en tu región?
2. ¿Cómo han cambiado a través del tiempo los organismos de tu región? ¿Encontraste apoyo para tu hipótesis? Explica.
3. ¿Que otra información encontraste sobre el clima o el ambiente en tu región durante el intervalo de tiempo que investigaste?

Saca conclusiones

1. Encuentra esta actividad de Usa Internet en el sitio Web de Glencoe Science science.glencoe.com. Compara tus datos con los de otros alumnos. Estudia los datos de otros alumnos para comparar información acerca de los períodos geológicos y fósiles que investigaste. Repasa los datos de otros alumnos acerca de los fósiles que investigaron.
2. Describe las plantas y animales fósiles que se han descubierto en tu región. ¿Qué pistas encontraste acerca de los ambientes de tus organismos fósiles? ¿Eran semejantes al ambiente en tu región en la actualidad?
3. Infiere de los organismos fósiles de tu región cómo pudo haber sido la geografía y el clima durante el intervalo de tiempo geológico que escogiste.

Guía de estudio

Repasa las ideas principales

Refiérete a las figuras de tu libro de texto.

Sección 1 La vida y el tiempo geológico

1. El tiempo geológico se divide en eones, eras, períodos y épocas.
2. Las divisiones dentro de la escala del tiempo geológico se basan en gran medida en cambios evolutivos importantes de los organismos.
3. Los movimientos de las placas causan cambios que afecta la evolución orgánica. *¿De qué forma la formación de montañas como las de abajo, puede afectar la evolución de las especies?*

Sección 2 Historia temprana de la Tierra

1. Las cianobacterias fueron una forma de vida temprana que evolucionó durante la Era Precámbrica. Los trilobites, peces y corales eran abundantes durante la Era Paleozoica.
2. Las plantas y animales comenzaron a invadir la tierra a mediados de la Era Paleozoica. Estas plantas y animales evolucionaron rápidamente y colonizaron la tierra.
3. La Era Paleozoica fue un tiempo de formación de montañas. Los montes Apalaches se formaron cuando varias islas y luego África chocaron con Norte América.
4. Al final de la Era Paleozoica, se extinguieron muchos invertebrados marinos. *¿Qué tipo de organismo marino se muestra aquí?*

Sección 3 Historia intermedia y reciente de la Tierra

1. Las formas terrestres dominantes durante la Era Mesozoica fueron los reptiles y las gimnospermas. Los mamíferos y las angiospermas comenzaron a dominar la tierra en la Era Cenozoica.
2. Pangaea se dividió durante la Era Mesozoica. Durante el Cenozoico se formaron muchas cadenas montañosas.
3. Homo sapiens apareció durante la época del Plioceno. *¿Cómo pudo contribuir Homo sapiens a la extinción de animales?*

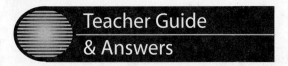

Hands-On Activities

MiniLab (page 3)

1. Layer 2; it contains fossils A and B. These fossil organisms lived together during the Ordovician Period.
2. There is only one fossil in each layer, and that fossil existed during two different periods.

MiniLab: Try at Home (page 4)

1. Student answers will depend on the points they chose on each continent and their measurements. Separations of 6,000 to 7,000 km would take from 160 to 200 million years to achieve.
2. Values should be in the range of 160 to 200 million years.

Activity (page 5)

Lab Preview

1. Ten times for creatures six to ten units tall, and six times for creatures eight to ten units tall.
2. Student answers will vary. Accept all reasonable answers.

Conclude and Apply

1. It increased.
2. No; the average would remain at about 6. The shortest varimals would still have been part of the calculation for the average height.
3. Some of the original varimals weren't able to obtain enough food to survive and, therefore, weren't able to reproduce.
4. This particular population would have become extinct.
5. Probably not; if all the individuals would have been the same height, no group of individuals would have had an advantage in reaching high food. In that case any evolution of the varimal population would likely have occurred from some variation of a trait other than height.
6. By creating the variation of a trait within the varimal population, in this case height, the model demonstrates how the species was able to evolve into one capable of reaching food high above the ground.

Activity: Use the Internet (page 7)

Analyze Your Data

Answers will be subjective and based on students' individual research.

Draw Conclusions

Answers will be individualized and often based on the students' opinion of his or her research. Look for depth and quality of research performed.

Laboratory Activity 1 (page 9)

Data and Observations

1. eye color, height, hair color, skin color—Students may think of others.

Table 1
Answers will vary.

Table 2
Answers will vary.

Questions and Conclusions

1. Height, upright walking, ability to communicate with each other with verbal and written languages are possible answers.
2. Answers will vary.
3. Answers will vary, but height should be somewhat shorter.
4. The members of the species have become taller.
5. By watching how one characteristic changes over time, scientists can date fossils.
6. The changes take place over a much longer time span (millions of years) when dealing with fossils.

Laboratory Activity 2 (page 11)

Lab Note: You may need to remind students that 1,000 million years equals 1 billion years.

Data and Observations

Table 1
Precambrian Time; 3.956 billion years or 3 billion, 956 million years
Paleozoic Era; 296 million years
Mesozoic Era; 183 million years
Cenozoic Era; 65 million years

Graph
Should show data accurately, making clear the enormous difference in the length of the Precambrian Era as compared with of the each of the other three Eras.

Timeline
Specific representations will vary slightly, but should clearly show the relative differences among the Eras. Art should be relative and pertinent to the Era with which it is associated.

Questions and Conclusions

1. Precambrian time is the longest division; the Cenozoic Era is the shortest division.
2. about 2.1 times longer
3. in the Cenozoic Era; in the Holocene Epoch
4. at least 30 times longer; exact answers will vary depending on numbers used for calculations.
5. Answers will vary, but might include that the most recent events were difficult to mark and illustrate because the time periods represent such a small part of the time line.

Meeting Individual Needs

Directed Reading for Content Mastery (page 17)

Overview
1. Paleozoic
2. Cenozoic
3. Mesozoic
4. Precambrian
5. Mesozoic
6. cyanobacteria
7. amphibians
8. Precambrian

Sections 1 and 2
1. eons
2. geologic time scale
3. species
4. natural selection
5. Paleozoic
6. periods
7. fossils
8. organic evolution
9. only a few
10. longest
11. blue-green
12. E
13. A
14. C
15. D
16. B

Section 3
1. present
2. dinosaurs
3. birds
4. angiosperms
5. *Homo Sapiens*
6. Pangaea
7. Alps and Himalayas
8. a
9. b

Key Terms
1. eras
2. trilobites
3. Precambrian
4. cyanobacteria
5. birds
6. Pangaea
7. epoch
8. Jurassic
9. geological time scale
10. eons
11. period
12. organic evolution
13. species
14. natural selection

Lectura dirigida para Dominio del contenido (pág. 21)

Sinopsis
1. Paleozoica
2. Cenozoica
3. Mesozoica
4. Precámbrico
5. Mesozoica
6. cianobacterias
7. anfibios
8. Precámbrico

Secciones 1 y 2
1. eones
2. escala del tiempo geológico
3. especie
4. selección natural
5. Paleozoica
6. períodos
7. fósiles
8. evolución orgánica
9. contienen sólo unos cuantos fósiles
10. más larga
11. azul verdosas
12. E
13. A
14. C
15. D
16. B

Sección 3
1. hace 65 millones de años
2. dinosaurios
3. aves
4. angiospermas
5. *Homo*
6. Pangaea
7. Alpes e Himalayas
8. a
9. b

Términos claves
1. era
2. trilobites
3. Precámbrico
4. cianobacterias
5. aves
6. Pangaea
7. época
8. Jurásico
9. escala del tiempo geológico
10. eones
11. períodos
12. evolución orgánica
13. especies
14. selección natural

Reinforcement (page 25)

Section 1
1. the types of life-forms and geologic events
2. Cenozoic era
3. To help describe Earth's past environments, to interpret how extinct organisms lived, to document changes in species.
4. Location on head, shape, and size relate to swimmers, predators, and surface dwellers.
5. They exhibit physical changes through time; many trilobite species lived for short periods of geologic time.
6. Change in climate, change in habitat, increase in predation.
7. The rearranging of land and sea causes changes in climate and terrain.
8. In order to live in water with low oxygen levels.
9. In water or moist places.
10. In the Recent epoch, Quaternary period, Cenozoic era.

Section 2
1. cyanobacteria
2. oxygen is major atmospheric gas
3. shielding of Earth from ultraviolet rays
4. complex organisms
5. invertebrates
6. organisms with hard parts
7. fish
8. amphibians
9. reptiles
10. Pangaea
11. #1–5; 6–10
12. Precambrian rocks have been deeply buried, changed by heat and pressure, and eroded. Many fossils can't withstand these processes.
13. Most Paleogoic life-forms lived in the ocean.
14. With the forming of Pangaea, oceans and landmasses changed and climates changed form mild and warm to cold and dry.

Section 3
1. f
2. h
3. e
4. k
5. d
6. a
7. q
8. j
9. p
10. b
11. g
12. l
13. i
14. o
15. c
16. m
17. rings similar to growth in trees
18. warm
19. nurtured

Enrichment (page 28)

Section 1
1. the conclusion that primates evolved only 60 million years ago
2. High Atlas is the name of the mountains where the fossils was found. *Alti* means "high," as in *alti*tude. *Atlas* is the second part of the mountain's name.
3. Student answers will vary. An important point is that scientists use new information to change existing theories.

Section 2
1. Cambrian: soft-bodied animals, marine animals with mineralized shells, such as trilobites, echinoderms, brachiopods, mollusks, and a variety of worms; Ordovician: graptolities, cephalopods, bryozoans, gastropods, bivalves, echinoids, and corals; Silurian: brachiopods, crinoids, corals, primitive fish; Devonian: various fish, including shark, lungfish, and armored fish; Carboniferous: most of Devonian forms plus Stegocephalia, a lizard-like amphibian, spiders, snails, and a dragonfly-like insect known as the Meganeura; Permian: lizard-like and semi-aquatic reptiles, cockroaches.
2. The absence of oxygen at the bottom prevented bacteria from decomposing the leaves. The leaves were covered with mud which later turned to rock in a dry lake bed.
3. Yes. Although many species, such as the blastoids and trilobites became extinct, the ammonoids, brachiopods, bryozoans, corals, and crinoids survived.
4. Answers will vary but students should note that background extinctions are part of a natural ongoing process.

Section 3
1. Golenberg discovered actual leaves. Most fossils of plants no longer contain the original organic material.
2. The absence of oxygen at the bottom prevented bacteria from decomposing the leaves. The leaves were covered with mud which later turned to rock in a dry lake bed.
3. Answers will vary. Some might say no—the red magnolia leaves indicate that the leaves probably turned shades of red and gold as they often do now. Others might say there simply isn't enough evidence to decide.

Note-taking Worksheet (page 31)
Refer to Teacher Outline, student answers are underlined.

Teacher Guide & Answers (continued)

Assessment

Chapter Review (page 35)

Part A. Vocabulary Review

1. reptiles (5/2)
2. amphibians (4/2)
3. invertebrates (4/2)
4. geologic time scale (1/1)
5. cyanobacteria (4/2)
6. species (4/2)
7. vertebrates (5/2)
8. angiosperms (4/2)
9. gymnosperms (7/3)
10. index fossil (2/1)
11. natural selection (5/2)

```
G E O L O G I C  T I M E S C A L E  V B
K D C Z B A J  Y  Q R E P T I L E S D M
V F M D K L T  A M P H I B I A N S X  I
T X K O R Y A  N O C E P O L L T M O  N
B X D G Y M N  O S P E R M S R X D R  D
I N V E R T E  B R A T E S  S Z J C K  E
M B Y F M Y R  A N G I O S P E R M S  X
X D F L V P P  C Q J D J Q E K Z M L  F
C H X B I B A  T K S A R D C F T K V  O
J Y K D Q D V  E V C F K F I Q B J C  S
M V E R T E B  R A T E S B E R A R T  S
B K A B K X Z  I P R B Z T S C S Z K  I
A Z N A T U R  A L S E L E C T I O N  U
```

Part B. Concept Review

1. It's divided into eons, which are further divided into eras, periods, and epochs. (1/1)
2. Cyanobacteria are though to be one of the earliest forms of life on Earth. Invertebrates developed near the end of the time. Jellyfish and marine worms also existed. (4/2)
3. The era began when organisms developed hard parts. Fish and other sea animals, amphibians, and reptiles dominated the era. Mass extinctions of many land and sea animals occurred at the end of the era. (6/2)
4. Pangaea separated into two large masses, then broke up further, forming the present-day continents. The change in land caused climates to change; thus new species that adapted to the different climates evolved. (8/1)
5. Humans first appeared during the Pleistocene epoch. (9/3)
6. Oxygen became a major gas in Earth's atmosphere, and the ozone layer in the stratosphere began to develop, shielding Earth from ultraviolet rays. (5/2)

Chapter Test (page 37)

I. Testing Concepts

1. c (1/1)
2. a (9/3)
3. d (1/1)
4. d (2/1)
5. c (7/3)
6. a (9/3)
7. a (5/2)
8. d (7/3)
9. a (5/2)
10. a (4/2)
11. c (4/2)
12. b (6/2)
13. b (7/3)
14. b (9/3)
15. d (2/1)
16. d (4/2)
17. d (3/1)
18. a (8/3)

II. Understanding Concepts

1. Plate tectonics changes Earth's environments. Species adapt to the changes or become extinct. (3/1)
2. The breaking up of Pangaea changed climates and habitats. One type of organism that adapted was the reptile. Dinosaurs evolved from reptiles. (8/3)
3. Competition with other species for food and overhunting might have led to the extinction of other mammals. (9/3)
4. Their seeds are protected and enclosed in a fruit, allowing them to develop in varied environments. (7/1)
5. evolution of cyanobacteria (4/2)
6. disappearance of Ediacaran fauna (5/2)
7. dinosaurs as dominant life-form (7/3)
8. development of birds (7/3)
9. appearance of humans (9/3)
10. **a.** Quarternary; Holocene, Pleistocene; humans appear (7/3)
    b. Tertiary; Pliocene, Miocene, Oligocene, Eocene, Paleocene; mammals abundant, angiosperms are dominant, dinosaurs were extinct (7/3)

III. Applying Concepts

1. As plates moved, continents collided with and separated from one another. This resulted in mountain building and the draining of seas, which caused changing environments. This process continues today. Thus species need to adapt to different environments. (3/1)
2. Little is known because rocks from the Precambrian time have been buried deeply and changed by heat and pressure. They have been eroded more than more recent rocks. These changes have affected the fossil record as well. In addition, early invertebrates were soft-bodied and not easily preserved as fossils. (2/1)
3. The reptile evolved an egg with a membrane that protected it from drying out. This enabled it to lay eggs in dry environments, rather than having to return to water to reproduce. (4/2; 6/2)
4. Mass extinctions of many land and sea animals occurred. These extinctions might have been caused when all the continental plates came together to form Pangaea, and the climate changed as a result. (6/2)
5. Until Earth was shielded from ultraviolet rays, most organisms couldn't survive when exposed to the Sun. (5/2)

6. Trilobites are marine animals. They were widespread during the Paleozoic era because seas covered much of Earth's surface then. Species of trilobites existed for short periods of time. (4/2)

7. Precambrian life had primarily soft parts; during the Paleozoic era, animals with hard parts evolved. (4/2)

8. They had common ancestors. (7/3)

9. Animal life in the Mesozoic era included marine life, amphibians, and reptiles. Dinosaurs were dominant by the Jurassic period. By the early Cenozoic era, dinosaurs and many other life-forms were extinct. Birds and mammals had evolved. (7/3)

Transparency Activities

Section Focus Transparency 1 (page 42)

Relatively Speaking...

Transparency Teaching Tips

- This is an introduction to geologic time. Explain that geologic time is based, in large part, upon the fossil record. Subdivisions of time (eons, eras, periods, and epochs) are differentiated by major worldwide changes, all of which are represented by the appearance and disappearance of animals in the fossil record.

- Point out that the fossil record is contained within the various layers of rock, as shown on the transparency. Take a small stack of books and a deck of playing cards. The cards represent animal species, and the books represent rock layers. Choose a dozen cards, some of the same type, and place each between the pages of the books, in some cases two or three being placed in different spots within the same book. Ask the students to explain how each card's placement in the stack reveals information as to first appearance, demise, and relative age. The cards represent animal species. The oldest cards are on the bottom, with the first card representing an animal's appearance. The last card represents the animal's disappearance, and the other cards between first and last represent animals that lived at the same time. This is how fossils within layers of rock reveal information about life on Earth.

Content Background

- The rock layers of the Vermillion Cliffs were laid down during the Jurassic Period, around 138 to 205 million years ago. Approximately five million years ago the Colorado River began caving out the Grand Canyon. Gradually, the river's waters, along with rain, wind, and melting snow, eroded rock layers, leaving the beautiful patterns shown on the transparency.

- The rock walls of the Vermillion Cliffs are made primarily of sandstone. Fossils within the cliffs' rock layers are millions of years old.

Answers to Student Worksheet

1. The layers were formed at different times. Each layer represents a different period of time.

2. The oldest layers are on the bottom. They were deposited first, while younger layers were laid over top.

3. Knowing the layers would reveal which fossil was oldest, how close in time they existed, and whether or not they might have coexisted.

Section Focus Transparency 2 (page 43)

An Early Plant

Transparency Teaching Tips

- You may use this transparency to introduce Earth's early history. Explain that Precambrian time is the section of the fossil record that dates back from 544 million to four billion years ago. It is the time when life first appeared. Few fossils have survived from this time, due to the simple forms of life present and the extreme heat and pressure applied to the rocks over the last four billion years.

- The Paleozoic Era came next, lasting from 544 until 245 million years ago. It is during this time that marine life (vertebrate and invertebrate), plants, insects, and the first reptiles appeared.

- Point out that the fossil shown on the transparency lived during the Silurian Period of this era, about 408 to 438 million years old. It is significant because *Cooksonia* may be the first vascular plant (a plant with tubes allowing the transport of water throughout the plant). It was a very successful plant, fossils being found in Ireland, England, Wales, Scotland, and Canada.

Content Background

- *Cooksonia* was a leafless, rootless, possibly vascular plant with a simple branching system and spore-producing organs on the tips. It was only a few centimeters in height (the fossil shown is 2.5 cm tall).

- *Cooksonia* became extinct in the next period, the Devonian Period, when land plants became abundant. Nevertheless, it was the forerunner of the vascular plants.

Answers to Student Worksheet

1. Students will probably indicate the stems or stalks of modern plants resemble *Cooksonia*.

2. Plants colonized land before animals. Without plants to produce food, life would be difficult for animals on land.

Section Focus Transparency 3 (page 44)

Big Smile for the Camera

Transparency Teaching Tips

- This transparency introduces the Mesozoic Era, Earth's middle history. Point out that following the

Paleozoic Era came the Mesozoic Era, the age of reptiles, approximately 240 to 65 million years ago.

■ At the beginning of the Mesozoic Era, the continents were joined in a single landmass. During this period, they gradually moved apart until they settled in their present locations. (They continue to move today.)

■ The first period of the Mesozoic Era, the Triassic (240 to 208 million years ago), saw the appearance of the first reptiles and small dinosaurs. A minor extinction occurred at the end of this period, with 35 percent of all animals dying. This cleared the way for dinosaurs.

■ The Jurassic Period came next (208 to 146 million years ago). This age saw the appearance of larger dinosaurs, such as Apatosaurus and Tyrannosaurus Rex, as well as birds, ferns, pine and gingko trees, and the ancestors of the shark pictured on the transparency.

■ The last period of the Mesozoic Era was the Cretaceous (146 to 65 million years ago). During this period, dinosaurs ruled, then died off. Ants, bees, crocodiles, and butterflies appeared, as did the first flowering plants.

■ Remind the students that the fossil record allows us to subdivide time into these eras and periods.

■ The Cenozoic Era began 65 million years ago and continues through today. It is our recent history and has been referred to as the age of mammals. The most recent period, the Quaternary (1.8 million years ago to the present) has been called the age of humans.

Content Background

■ The great white shark (*Carcharodon carcharias*) ranges in size up to 6.4 m (21 feet) and 3,300 kg (7,300 lbs). While known for its unprovoked and sometimes deadly attacks on human beings, the great white does not hunt humans specifically. In fact, more people were killed by dogs last year in the United States than by great whites in the last 100 years combined.

■ Megalodon, a possible ancestor of the great white (or at least a close relation), was a gigantic shark similar to the great white in anatomy and behavior. Because only fossilized teeth and vertebrae have ever been found, it is difficult to ascertain Megalodon's true size. Teeth of over 17 cm (6.5 inches) have been discovered, putting the shark at no less than 12 m (40 feet) and possibly up to 31 m (100 feet) in length! Megalodon was large enough to swallow a present-day great white whole. It became extinct roughly 1.6 million years ago.

Answers to Student Worksheet

1. Dinosaurs were the dominant land animals.

2. Sharks survived the events that caused the extinction of the dinosaurs on land. Modern sharks have survived from the Jurassic Period with relatively few changes, so they are similar to their fossilized ancestors.

3. Answers will vary. Possibilities include reptiles like crocodiles, lizards, and turtles.

Teaching Transparency (page 45)

Geologic Time Scale

Section 1

Transparency Teaching Tips

■ Explain that the geologic time scale is not divided into equal units. Rather, the time scale is determined by the time interval between significant geologic events.

■ Indicate to students that the intervals shown on the transparency are not to scale. Point out that if all of geologic time were one year, the Paleozoic Era would extend 47 days, the Mesozoic 14 days, and the Cenozoic 5 days. Humans would have appeared only on the last day of the year. Precambrian time would take up the remainder of the year.

Reteaching Suggestion

■ Suggest students prepare a geologic time scale for the classroom using adding machine tape or strips of paper. Have them illustrate their time scale with pictures from magazines or drawings.

Extensions

Activity: Have pairs of students trace the development of one group of organisms identified on the geologic time scale (e.g. land plants, marine invertebrates, reptiles, or birds). Ask the students to compile photos or drawings to show the development of the organism. Have them prepare a poster or other display for the class.

Challenge: Encourage interested students to trace the geologic history of one landform of Pangaea. Suggest they present their findings to the class as a visual report.

Answers to Student Worksheet

1. era, period, epoch

2. Precambrian rocks have been buried so deeply that they have been changed by heat and pressure. Also, Precambrian organisms didn't have hard parts, so their chance to be fossilized would be decreased.

3. 85 million years; Pennsylvanian

4. Paleozoic era; Devonian period.

5. No, fish appeared over 40 million years ago, so the fossil would not be unusual.

6. Yes, the Permian Period was 286 million years ago, the first birds appeared during the Jurassic Period, 200 million years later.

Assessment Transparency (page 47)

Geologic Time

Section 3

Answers

1. **B.** This question requires students to correctly read the table and see that dinosaurs appeared during the *Mesozoic Era.*
2. **J.** Students must carefully read the question and the table to determine which time period existed more than 800 million years ago. The only time period on the table that occurred that long ago was the *Precambrian Era.*
3. **C.** Students must carefully read the table and infer that frogs are amphibians and since amphibians first appeared during the *Paleozoic Era,* choice C is the correct answer.

Test-Taking Tip
Encourage students to be extra careful in their reading when the questions and answers contain words that are difficult to pronounce.

A Division of The McGraw·Hill Companies

ISBN 0-07-825394-2

90000

 **Glencoe McGraw-Hill**

9 780078 253942